Jump, Puppy!

Susan B. Neuman

NATIONAL GEOGRAPHIC

Washington, D.C.

This is my puppy. Let's play.

Jump, puppy!

Tug!

Run.

Roll.

Catch a ball!

Catch a stick!

Wag your tail.

What can you smell?

What can you see?

Let's go for a walk.

Let's see some friends.

Lie in the sun.

Yawn!

Take a nap.

YOUR TURN!

Tell a story about a puppy.

Browse the complete Collins catalogue at
www.collins.co.uk

A catalogue record for this publication is available from the British Library.

ISBN: 978-0-00-826657-8
US Edition ISBN: 978-1-4263-1508-4

Book design by David M. Seager

Photo Credits

Cover, Tierfotoagentur/Alamy; 1, Close Encounters of the Furry Kind/Kimball Stock; 2–3, Gary Randall/Kimball Stock;
4, Jean-Michel Labat/ARDEA; 5, Jean-Michel Labat/ARDEA; 6, Renee Morris Animal Collection/Alamy; 7, Jean-Michel Labat/ARDEA;
8, Klein-Hubert/Kimball Stock; 9, Johan De Meester/ARDEA; 10–11, Stefanie Krause-Wieczorek/Imagebroker/Biosphoto; 12–13,
Jean-Michel Sotto/Kimball Stock; 14–15, Jean-Michel Labat/ARDEA; 16, John Daniels/ARDEA; 17, Close Encounters of the Furry Kind/
Kimball Stock; 18–19, Close Encounters of the Furry Kind/Kimball Stock; 20–21, Ron Kimball/Kimball Stock; 22, Gary Randall/Kimball
Stock; 23 (top), John Daniels/ARDEA; 23 (puppy), John Daniels/ARDEA; 23 (ball), Stepan Bormotov/Shutterstock; 23 (bottom),
Jean-Michel Labat/ARDEA; 24, Sabine Steuwer/Kimball Stock

Printed and bound in China by RR Donnelley APS